It's Not About Me

How to win with servant leadership

By Bob and Austin Hintze

Copyright © 2017 Waypoint Property Inspection. All rights reserved. No portion of this book may be reproduced mechanically, electronically, or by any other means, including photocopying, without written permission of the publisher. It is illegal to copy this book, post it to a website, or distribute it by any other means without permission from the publisher.

Limits of Liability and Disclaimer of Warranty

The author and publisher shall not be liable for your misuse of this material. This book is strictly for informational and educational purposes.

Warning – Disclaimer

The purpose of this book is to educate and entertain. The author and/or publisher do not guarantee that anyone following these techniques, suggestions, tips, ideas, or strategies will become successful. The author and/or publisher shall have neither liability nor responsibility to anyone with respect to any loss or damage caused or alleged to be caused, directly or indirectly by the information contained in this book.

Edited by Anaik Alcasas

Dedication- This book is dedicated to our loving family who truly knows the definition of unwavering support.

Epigraph – "Good leaders must first become good servants."

Robert K. Greenleaf

Contents

Foreword 7

Introduction 10

CHAPTER 1: SURVIVING CORPORATE ROCK BOTTOM (BOB'S STORY) 15

CHAPTER 2: THE BELIZE HOLIDAY EPIPHANY 20

    The Captain, the Tour Guide, the Chef 23

    Servant Leadership = Personalized Attention 25

    Servant Leadership = Ongoing Service 26

    Servant Leadership = Enabling Goal Achievement 27

CHAPTER 3: HOW TO BOOST YOUR BUSINESS 31

    Open Up to Young Blood (Austin's story) 32

    Communicate Your Why 36

    Collaborate with the Competition 42

    Operate as a Team 49

CHAPTER 4: HOW TO CONNECT WITH YOUR CLIENTS 54

    Combine Excellence with Diplomacy 54

    Write Hard and Talk Soft 60

    Offer a 200-Percent Guarantee 65

Champion Causes in Your Community 67

Build Lifelong Client Relationships 72

Conclusion 74

Acknowledgments 78

Contact the Authors 79

Foreword

Be Successful... and Be Around Those That Are Successful, because the more money you make, the more people you can help. Bob, Eddy, and Austin are a true inspiration to anyone that has been kicked to the curb by the corporate world. I have seen it happen to so many people and have to come to realize that it is a soul crusher. If you have experienced this, then this story is for you.

For those of you that believe in delivering a service – in fact approaching your business with a servant heart instead of being the "Stud" of the industry, then this book is for you.

For those of you that embrace family as you are becoming successful – especially when that family includes your children, then this book is for you.

In fact, this book, in my humble opinion, is for everyone that wants to "help people help themselves and others" – which is part of why I believe we are all on this planet... to help each other.

As you read the story that starts with Bob, then includes his brother-in-law Eddy and eventually includes his amazing son Austin, you will see that they have learned to move from what most would have termed a disaster to one incredible success after another. Even better with the stories and their complete honesty, you will also see how you can apply the same kind of success to your life and your business, especially as you understand their why and more importantly "YOUR WHY". I suspect the two will cross and most likely you will see a direct comparison from their story to your story. I know I do.

I also left the corporate world when I saw that the company I was working for was losing the battle with our competition. It was a knee-shaking day for me, and I wondered how I was going to be able to support my family. Like Bob – I was fortunate to have a loving wife that supported me through the change and still does today. We all should be so blessed. On top of that, I also have been blessed by all of my children working with me in the company at one point or another.

Honestly, I am not sure who to sympathize with the most The Father or The Son... I have been on both sides of the coin, and I know they face many challenges as they both continue to grow. Don't we all. So take a moment and take an exciting journey with a couple of special people that are willing to share with you how they continue to become more successful and you will be all the better for it. I plan to hang around them for a long time to come, and I hope both of my oldest who still work with me will have the chance to hang around Austin as they all grow into what the world is unfolding to them.

Then maybe you can also...

Be Successful... and Be Around Those That Are Successful

Mike Crow - Millionaire Inspector Community Founder

Introduction

Waypoint Property Inspection had its humble beginnings as a one-man home-based business known as "Bob's" Inspections. It has grown over the last twelve years into a family business – Bob, his son Austin and brother-in-law Eddy – serving west central Florida.

Since 2013 business revenue has more than tripled, and we have grown to a team of thirteen, with Austin doing a phenomenal job with marketing, brand building, and relationship building.

To date, Waypoint inspectors have completed well over 9000 full home inspections and specialty inspections throughout the Greater Tampa area, and we fully expect to be a one million dollar company within the next year.

In recent times our business success has shifted our entire paradigm and focus from merely providing the most excellent home inspections available (something our team still does) to coming alongside other real estate industry professionals, including Realtors©, as colleagues and consultants.

People have asked us to explain just how we've seen such tremendous gains in our business, including the strategic partnerships we've formed with other professionals in the real estate industry and how we've been able to take our collaborations to the next level.

In particular, people are fascinated by the language, motivations, and procedures around our servant leadership approach. People wonder, "what does servant leadership look like? How do you train your team in servant leadership? How do you hire new team members with servant leadership values in mind? How does servant leadership ensure clients remain loyal for life?" We answer these questions and more throughout this book with case studies, personal encounters, and hard-won lessons we learned on our journey.

A large part of our servant leadership approach now involves mentorship and training through the presentations we schedule throughout the year. This means that while we had to knock on a lot of doors in years past, now we're invited to provide coaching and consultant roles in the real estate community. While in times past we just provided the basic inspection service, making us a minor part of the property transaction, now we're an equal part of the transaction, and our real estate partners and colleagues rely on us for our expertise outside of the home inspection.

We get calls from Realtors© asking for our expert advice in order to help their transactions move along, even when we're not involved in those particular transactions.

This book has been written in particular to share insights into how you as an industry professional – whether in your own inspection business or in your real estate business – can boost your business and connect with your home buyers and sellers on an entirely new level.

Chapter 1: Surviving Corporate Rock Bottom, gives you a little insight into Waypoint's founder Bob Hintze and the circumstances that drove him – like many of you – to launch his own business.

Chapter 2: The Belize Holiday Epiphany, provides insight into the holiday family getaway that crystallized for Bob and Austin just how important the servant leadership approach can be, as they were dazzled by the next-level service approach of their Belize hosts and tour guides.

Chapter 3: How to Boost Your Business, distills some of the most crucial servant leadership lessons that have resulted in Waypoint's astronomical business growth, including the importance of opening up to young blood (the story of how and why Austin joined the team), how and when to communicate your "why" to captivate your audience, and the secrets of finding your tribe, collaborating with the competition, and operating as a team.

Chapter 4: How to Connect with Your Clients, continues in the servant leadership vein, going into more detail on Waypoint's methods for building lifelong client relationships, the irresistible draw of a 200-percent guarantee, how to write hard and talk soft when it comes to property transactions, how to nudge from behind and operate in a mentor capacity to those who seek out your advice and property expertise, and finally (because what you care about shows what kind of company you're running) the benefits of championing causes in your community.

Packed with both stories and insights, this book is also handy should you ever get a chance to work with Waypoint, as our values, standards, and motivations are explained from the inside out. We hope through this book you'll see that we're dedicated to bringing our best game to ensure a professional, high-integrity transaction that helps you look good!

You'll walk away from this book with two things: the insights, insider tips, stories, and real-life examples to help you grow into even more success in your own business, as well as a fundamental paradigm shift in which you learn to communicate both your excellence and your passion from the heart as opposed to just trying to impress people with your job title and track record.

CHAPTER 1: SURVIVING CORPORATE ROCK BOTTOM (BOB'S STORY)

In 1997 I had a great job in the corporate world. I was traveling throughout the South and Southwest meeting great people and coaching them. I was on cloud nine. I had an infant son, who is now 22 years old, and a loving wife. Things seemed to be going well.

In the course of five minutes all that came crashing down to the earth. I was in my office one day, and my boss walked in, and five minutes later I was out of a job.

I remember leaning against my car in the parking lot. I was lost and didn't know what to do. I felt like I let everybody, especially my family, down.

For a while, I couldn't focus. I was in a fog. I really didn't have a plan. One day after picking up my son Austin from daycare, I went and picked up my wife, Jeannette. She got in the car, saw the lost look on my face and said, "Whatever you want to do next, I support you 100 percent!" I think back upon that moment a lot now — losing my job was like getting hit in the face with a cold slap, but then it was followed by a warm, loving embrace through my wife's assurance. Basically, I was told, "Wake up Bob! Get your act together but know that you've got a big support system behind you."

I got my confidence back, I worked hard. I got another job in corporate finance. Worked my way up and did really well. Then in mid-2004 my company held a big meeting and said: "within six months you're all going to be out of a job." I was offered other positions in the company, but I didn't want to relocate my family, which I had done several times before. It was a sad day in late 2004 when I had to shake the hands of 500 people as I was laying them off and then subsequently follow them out the door a few months later.

What will I do next? I did some soul searching. I really looked back upon my life up to that point and said, "Bob, what have you done that you feel you've done well?" When I was playing soccer as a kid, I became the team captain. In high school, I was president of the key club where we were known for our community assistance. In college, I became a resident advisor, an RA, and was the leader of my dormitory. The common theme of my life experiences involved leading others and encouraging others.

Taking that theme, I found that home inspection was a way that I could really help others. I could lead and educate others, and I didn't have to have 500 people directly reporting to me like I did in the corporate world.

So I thought, home inspecting is a good career where I could be one-on-one with my customers and clients, whether they're real estate agents or folks that are buying or selling a home. I could be a leader in this field, and guide clients and help them achieve what they'd like to achieve – whether it is a smooth transaction for Realtors© or peace of mind for new home owners.

In 2005 I formed Waypoint Property Inspection, also known as "Bob's Inspections," and was a one man shop until early 2013. Business has been good since the start. We've never had a down year, and that includes those years where the real estate market went bust. I am proud to say, I was able to be a full-time home inspector from 2005 to 2013. My business had steady growth and was doing well.

Then in early 2013, my brother-in-law, Eddy, left his corporate job and joined me as an inspector. He also became part owner of the company. During the year, business was good; our schedules were often over-filled. We were working seven days a week and had to make a decision. Should we stay a two-man shop and be very, very busy, turning business away, or grow Waypoint into something bigger? We decided to grow because it felt like the right thing to do, and it was.

Today we have an office, seven inspectors, support staff, marketing staff, trainees and our business is growing by leaps and bounds.

CHAPTER 2: THE BELIZE HOLIDAY EPIPHANY

In December 2015, Jeannette, Austin and I took a long overdue family vacation. We were looking to get away somewhere in Central or South America. While looking at a map, our fingers fell upon Belize because although we didn't know much about it, we'd heard it was a beautiful country.

We took a flight on a national carrier into the airport in Belize City. When we landed, we found out that our luggage was still in Miami and was not going to make it to

Belize until later in the day due to an issue we had back in the States.

With the news about our missing luggage hanging over us, we were greeted by a friendly Belizean, and from that moment on, our hands were being held every step of the way, figuratively speaking and almost literally. We took a very small four-seater plane from Belize City into San Pedro, a little town on the island of Ambergris Caye. I was worried that our luggage wasn't going to make it.

Here we were in this tropical environment, slightly uncomfortable and not properly dressed for the weather. But while we were worried, we were in good spirits and hopeful. We checked into the resort, and folks were just bending over backwards to make us comfortable and assured us they would take care of everything. We settled into our casita and just a few hours later, our luggage made it to us after arriving in Belize City.

Somebody had hand carried our luggage from Belize City to one of the small planes destined for San Pedro, and then our resort staff brought it from the airport directly to our casita. We were immensely impressed not just by the service but by the sincerity behind it.

When you lose your luggage, or it is misplaced in the United States, you're lucky if you get it the next day or get it at all. So right away we knew that our experience in Belize would be something special.

For our holiday we had signed up with a company that provides certain tours over a number of days. One of the trips scheduled was to visit the Mayan ruins deep in the Belizean rain forest. Early one morning we flew to a town called Orange Walk in northern Belize. As we flew in, we saw a small runway with one building surrounded by miles and miles of sugar cane fields and somebody standing next to a pickup truck. Obviously, this was not the kind of experience you would have in the States.

The Captain, the Tour Guide, the Chef

We got out of the little plane, and a man named Alberto was there to personally pick us up. He waved to us, and we went over and hopped into his truck. Alberto was very talkative, introduced himself, and took us to a small outpost on the New River where we got into his boat – the tour started well north of the ruins – and we proceeded to navigate on a 22 mile winding ride through the interior of the country.

Alberto was our captain and focused on different points of interest, including Monkey Island, a unique cactus that looks like a snake and several Mennonite farms. We also learned more about him and his family, especially his children. He used to work in Belize City, about an hour and a half away from his home in Orange Walk, but it was too much of a drive, and he wanted to be near his family.

When we got to the Mayan ruins, Alberto became our tour guide. It wasn't just a case of the boat guy drops you off, and then somebody else picks you up and takes over. Alberto was with us from start to finish. There were other bigger tour companies at the ruins where they had dozens of people with just one tour guide. Meanwhile, we had this personalized service from Alberto. We toured the different ruins, went to the top of the largest ruins and took panoramic pictures, all the while having Alberto share the history and information. It was really enjoyable and also a true learning experience.

To top it off, when we were done Alberto actually made us lunch. It wasn't, "Okay, let's stop at McDonald's," or, "Let's bring in the bagged fast food." Albert literally made and served us the country staple, which is chicken and rice with beans. It was absolutely delicious because it was homemade. He made sure that we had plenty of food and he gave us a choice of what we wanted to drink, which in Belize is very interesting because they have colas that we haven't seen in years in the States.

After finishing lunch, we navigated the New River back to Orange Walk, got into the pickup truck, and went to the airport. While waiting for our plane, we sat with Alberto for a while, talked more, and learned more. Then in the distance, we saw this little six-seater plane come into view and again, land on that small runway in the middle of a sugar cane field. We said our goodbyes to Alberto and took off back to Ambergris Caye.

Servant Leadership = Personalized Attention

I'm sure Alberto provides this level of personalized service every day, but he made us feel like he was doing this tour with us for the very first time by the attention, care and personal interest he put into every moment with us. It reminded us that in business, even though we have numerous clients each day, most times we are only performing our services once in front of a particular client. You only have one chance to make an impression and to do it right for each client.

Servant Leadership = Ongoing Service

From the moment we met Alberto, he was with us every step of the journey and made sure that our every need was fulfilled under his care. He was our leader.

That's who we are at Waypoint Property Inspection with regards to the customers and clients that we serve. Our commitment is to provide an experience just like Alberto provided. He was there to meet our plane, drove us to the boat, piloted the boat, saw us onto shore, led us through the Mayan ruins, furnished us with relevant information all throughout our time together, fed us and ensured we were comfortable. Our goal at Waypoint is for the care to be ongoing start to finish, basically for as long as the client wants it. In some cases, it's years of ongoing service. We have clients that we served years ago that still count on us. Yes, we provide home inspections and reports, but we do a lot more than that. We really are in the client care and relationship business, we just happen to inspect homes.

Servant Leadership = Enabling Goal Achievement

To expound on the definition of servant leadership, we run our business through the filter of helping each person achieve their unique goals. Whoever we have the privilege of working with, whether it's a Realtor©, a client buying a house, a client selling a house, or anyone needing additional services – whoever is in front of us – we truly are committed to helping them achieve their goals.

We don't necessarily define their goals for them. Going back to Alberto, he didn't define what our goals were. Our goals were: we wanted to see Mayan ruins and take a boat ride. But he did furnish the experience.

Our buyers wish to buy a house, but what we do is much more like Alberto; he brought the experience of being a caregiver, somebody who is very knowledgeable, somebody who you could see really, <u>truly enjoyed helping us and serving us.</u>

That's what we do as a company.

Since leaving corporate America in 2004 and starting Waypoint Property Inspection, client service, and client satisfaction has always been a part of who I am, who Waypoint is, always making sure that we provide top notch service and a sincere experience.

We knew we were already doing that in our business because of our client feedback, reviews and the referrals we received. The trip to Belize helped us define "why" we were doing it (more on that later in the book.) We're focused on our clients' and business partners' needs 100%, and we have now moved into educator and advocate roles in the industry. At the end of the day we're thinking about what we accomplished, but more than that we're thinking about who we helped.

Not every business does that. The day before yesterday a Realtor© who we have a close relationship with called me early in the afternoon. She was a little distraught. One of her home buyers just had an inspection with a different inspection company, and the experience didn't go well. The buyers were very detail-oriented, and they basically wanted everything gone over "with a fine tooth comb." But when they asked the inspector to go beyond normal protocol, he responded that he'd only follow the inspection standards. Technically his response wasn't wrong but it didn't match the client's expectations. If you go into the industry inspection standards, they state, "Inspect a representative sample of X, inspect a representative sample of Y." So they were asking the inspector to do certain things that a home inspector doesn't necessarily have to do.

Now this request was just one part of what our Realtor© colleague called us about, and it's possible the inspector was just having a bad day. I know the company, and I know the owner of the company. He was not the inspector; it was one of his employees that was doing the job. It reminded me how important it is to make sure your service exceeds your client's goals and expectations.

The secret to explosive business success is to approach every client relationship saying, "How can I serve these people? What are these people's goals? How can we exceed them?"

In this particular case, with these detail-oriented home buyers, our approach would have been, "If you can get to it, then you should be able to inspect it, regardless of what the standards say." That's how we feel. We have a standard, that's baseline and is useful to ensure quality control. But all of our inspections exceed the baseline standards. That's our minimum goal.

In this case, our Realtor© friend called us to salvage the situation because she was at risk of losing the deal on the house, and potentially losing her clients. So we went in, and we did what we do every day, and in the end, they were extremely satisfied with our work and purchased the home. We walked away feeling good about the way we left the situation. Were we the saviors? No, but we were a partner in the solution. We played a vital role in meeting the home buyers' needs and goals.

CHAPTER 3: HOW TO BOOST YOUR BUSINESS

Others have asked us to educate them on how to provide high level of peace of mind to their clients and partners, and how to ensure that they are exceeding their clients' expectations. When you consistently exceed expectations, your business does experience success and growth, but how do you get that kick-start that will boost your business in the long term?

We recommend taking a holistic approach to your business that encompasses what kind of people you hire, what kind of motivations you communicate to others, what kind of mentors and partners you collaborate with, and how you foster the right kind of values as a team.

Open Up to Young Blood (Austin's story)

Companies that have been around for years or decades have the benefit of experience and longevity in the industry, but sometimes the leadership naturally gets a little defensive about the prospect of letting in anyone who's younger, with their high energy and new ideas. But we discovered that infusion of younger blood into Waypoint was symbiotic with the progress we wanted to make.

In 2014, while still in college, Austin agreed to join the company as our part-time marketing representative. Having him come on board and grow into a leadership role is a part of our strategy to grow into a million dollar and more company. Here is the story of his evolution from marketing rep to director of business development, in his own words:

I started out in high school as a shy kid who didn't have a place, until I decided to join the ROTC (Reserve Officer Training Corps) program. I worked my way up through the ROTC structure, assisting the other cadets and growing into more leadership roles. In my senior year of high school, I was actually the commander of the ROTC program which meant providing leadership and guidance to 250 high school cadets. After graduating high school, I got my first job in retail during my freshman year of college, working at a big box store. I pretty much held every position in that store and the last one involved working in the furniture department. All the windows were at the front of the store, and I was in the back of the store, which meant that I never saw outside when I was working.

I remember one night, in particular, I was the only one overseeing the furniture department and there were about five or six other employees in the store who were doing nothing. The store was basically empty. I remember the manager specifically singling me out to go and collect carts in the parking lot in the middle of a thunderstorm.

For those of you who don't live in Florida, we are notorious for our afternoon, nasty thunderstorms. So I was out there in the parking lot collecting these carts, getting soaking wet from the rain and it struck me that my position at this big box store was in stark contrast to what I was doing in my senior year of high school. What I was doing in this job was not appreciated; the company didn't appear to appreciate or respect me and the managers did not appreciate my work. I didn't have the feeling as though I was making a difference.

That's when I decided that I needed to turn things around. I've found that getting involved in the family business allows more freedom than a retail job environment and it provides more opportunity for impact. At Waypoint I feel like I'm making more of a contribution than I did before in that other job. I'm now in a position where I'm educating others about home inspections, and also more holistically, how to be successful and how to have a positive outlook. As the Director of Business Development, I also mitigate the issues that come up, and my role includes ensuring that people have a positive experience when working with us.

As far as being the young blood in the company, it's taken some time to grow strong relationships with our clients and business partners. A big part of my role is presenting regular workshops, going through exercises with Realtors© and teaching them how to better connect with home buyers (we cover this more in the next chapter.) I show them how to make an emotional connection and how to make their target audience feel that the information they're getting is going to benefit their lives in some way. A big part of what I teach also involves how to be more successful and how to have a different perspective.

It might be easy to back down and think, who am I to be telling them this? Who is this little 22 year old who just graduated college who doesn't really have that much of an insight on what they're going through? Although none of us can ever have complete insight into what our target audience is going through, we all bring a unique and different perspective on things.

The takeaway is that it doesn't matter if there are people in your audience or your ideal client group who are two or three decades, or more, your senior; you still have information to share that can make an impact on their lives. After working with some of my own mentors, coaches and communication experts I look up to, I decided that if just one person in that room comes out feeling better about their life, better about themselves, better about their business, then that's all that matters.

Communicate Your Why

Your success is paramount on knowing your *why*. Every month we host and teach training sessions with brand new real estate agents. It's never the same agents twice in these meetings. And with a recent group we decided to do a *why* exercise with them, which starts with a very basic question, "Why do you do what you do?" Now, often when people begin to try to express this, they just say, "Oh, it's for the money," or, "It's for the happiness," or, "It's for more free time," or other very basic answers.

But with this group of new agents we tried to get them into a bit of self-awareness, helping them to fully understand and then communicate why they're in this business and why they're doing the things that they are doing.

This concept of "begin with *why*" was introduced by a man named Simon Sinek in a TED talk. The example Sinek had shared during this TED talk was about Apple that had experienced amazing success as a company because they talked about "why they do what they do" before they talked about what they do and how they do it. Beginning with their *why* had helped Apple connect with people in a much more profound and effective way.

As the agents began sharing, one story, in particular, stood out. A woman in her late fifties started her *why* exercise with wanting to be closer to her children and her grandchildren. As we dug deeper and deeper into this exercise, she was opening up about how they're going through some rough times right now, and she wants to be closer to them to be able to support them. She wants to be able to guide them, help them and provide support to them.

I told her, "Now when you connect with a client who is trying to move closer to their child or a child trying to move closer to their parent, how powerful is it for you to know that your personal *why* is aligned with the clients you are serving?"

This is why it's so important to figure out your *why* and dig down deep, so that when you're out there helping people, you can begin to see them as much more than your clients. You begin to see them as people with similar goals and similar desires as yourself.

Those of us in the real estate industry might have come from other industries, like retail for example, where the customers are just going in, buying something off the shelf, and then they're out of there. The customers often have minimal significant ongoing connection with anybody who works in that field. Whereas the field that we work in, real estate, is very personal and it's very interactive.

Everything you do in this type of business involves being a good communicator. So it's important to do the *why* exercise in order to set the foundation for developing those personal connections. You're not just providing a one-off service, and that's it, it goes much deeper than that.

As a Realtor©, you can talk to your clients all day about the sales you've achieved, the houses you've sold, and this and that, but it's only when you find out your clients wants and needs, and change the structure of your communication process, that you can start to see the business boost that you're seeking.

The goal is to connect and build a genuine rapport with your potential clients, and that's not done by starting with what you do and how you do it. People don't care, because until they connect with you emotionally, they're really just thinking about "What's in it for me?"

So your *why* and why you're doing what you're doing is more important than what you're doing, who you're doing it with, what company you are and what service you provide. In the past at Waypoint we might have inundated our audience with dry facts such as, "I'm Austin with Waypoint Property Inspection, we've been in business since 2005, we've done X number of inspections, we have X many inspectors," and within 5 minutes you would see the first of many dozing off.

But turning it around, starting with the *why*, including why I am who I am, why I'm there to speak to them, and why I'm there to give them good information, I've seen a lot of head nods and people making direct eye contact and just seeming generally interested in the material.

The secret to sharing your *why* is starting out with a story that has a high-low-high pattern. You can't just come out with your *why* because people don't have any context about your current successes. So to start you tell them that things are going pretty well right now, this is the cool stuff I've been doing. You then turn to a low story that conveys things haven't always been this great. You talk about a very specific low point in your life and, particularly, the turning point that makes you decide you needed to turn things around. After the low story, you come back with another high story on how it's impacted you and what relation it has to the group you are speaking to.

When you're relating your *why* story, it's not so much a "Look at how great my life is," or trying to brag about your life. Rather you're sharing some of the trying times that have made you better as a person and how you've taken those lessons that you've learned and assimilated them in a way that can benefit them.

For example, part of Austin's low story is working in that big box store where they didn't care about any of the employees. I guarantee many people in your target audience have had jobs in the past where they felt devalued as an employee. So part of what you're doing with your story is building a connection point where the people in that room can connect with who you are as a person, what you were before, and what you're trying to be now and how that's going to help them in their own lives.

Really you're taking a lesson that you learned from the hard times that everyone can identify with and tying that into your reason for being on the platform speaking to them, sharing valuable insights to help the listeners get over their own hurdles and achieve what they want.

We've discovered that we have the highest and best engagement with our target audience when we share what our motivations are and what our beliefs are. No other home inspection company in our area that we know of is doing that. They're out there saying, "We have these services, and that's why you should use us because we do a great job, we love you, we love your clients." In a sense, that speak is coming from the head, not the heart.

Once you build that interest as a person, then you can build that into why you're actually there and what you're doing as a company, as a business, and what you're there to provide them. But they have to be interested in you as a person before they're going to care about what you're doing as a company or how you're doing it before they're likely to want to do business with you.

Collaborate with the Competition

We've had a couple fellow home inspectors who own companies pass away suddenly in the past few years. One was a good friend and fellow business owner, John, who lived in Colorado. He was part of a coaching group that Waypoint is part of. One day he had an accident at an inspection and went to the hospital. We thought everything would be okay but the next day he had an aneurysm as a result of a fall and he passed away. It was devastating to his wife and his daughter. His daughter worked with him in the business. Unfortunately, another fellow business owner from the Northeast passed away as well.

If that had happened to Waypoint prior to 2013, the business would have shut down- disappeared. Nobody would have been there to help carry it on. Back then Waypoint was just a one-man-shop. When it came to the business of home inspection, it was just me, "Bob's Inspections." The business was continuing to take off, and seeing steady growth but it was getting to be too much. I used to joke with people and tell them if I had another year like 2012 where it was just me, I'd have a lot of money in the bank, but I would be eating my meals through a straw because it was a crazy year and I knew I couldn't do it again by myself. I was working myself hard, and it was affecting my health and focus. I was an accident waiting to happen.

Up until that time, I'd probably gone to at least a dozen annual inspection conferences. It's all about learning more. It's all about getting better because in the end, the folks you serve will gain the positive outcome of what you learn and how you apply it. I'd been learning a lot, but at the same time, I was resisting the idea of joining a larger inspector community with other company owners.

I sat in on numerous sessions hosted by a prominent industry coach, Mike Crow. He's the head of the Millionaire Inspector Community or MIC. Mike's goal is to help at least 100 home inspection companies become million dollar businesses. I would leave each session thinking I'm doing well on my own and don't need anyone's help, especially Mike's.

Then in 2013 Eddy and I went to a conference in Las Vegas and heard Mike Crow again, and that was a turning point. I heard the same message that I had heard many times before but this time I felt it, Mike touched my heart. We decided at that point we were going to take Waypoint to the next level and joined MIC. We hired a marketer and our third inspector. We hired a call center because we were tired of taking calls in the attic and on the roof and we were losing business; potential clients got our voice mail and moved on to the next company.

We implemented the road map that Mike provided, and we followed it to a 'T'.

That was the starting point of going from a business that was steadily improving, year over year, with gains of five and ten percent to a business that is expanding with 35 to 50 percent year over year gains. Having a mentor and receiving help from a larger community of home inspection companies was one of the best decisions we have made and has helped Waypoint become the business it is today.

There are some great companies that are part of MIC, and we all get together several times a year to brainstorm. What are we doing well? Where could we all improve? We share best practices to enable all of us to be successful.

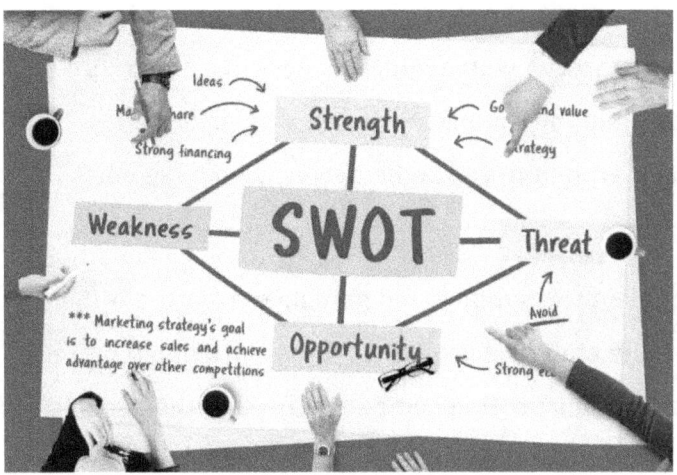

I see MIC as a team. Everybody is out to help everybody. For us, it's meant learning from the best. It's a community that is out to help each other, which ties into Waypoint's core principles of having a servant's heart. Mike and MIC's whole being is to help others succeed.

The two inspectors that had recently passed were also members of the Millionaire Inspector Community. After John's passing, the MIC community stepped up and went to his family and said, "We are not going to let you fail. We will do everything we can to make sure your business is successful." I sleep well at night knowing that if anything ever happened to me, Mike, the MIC team, and my MIC inspection partners would not let Waypoint fail.

As business leaders, we obviously expect to be around for a long time, but we never know what's going to happen tomorrow. What about you? If something were to happen to you tomorrow, would your business disappear? Do you have a community in place, people who give you feedback, who help you to be better, who have your back?

We've taken the support and guidance from the MIC community and have grown Waypoint into much more than a home inspection company. Through the regular presentations we hold and the training workshops we host, we try to make it clear that we're there to partner with each agent we work with, thus providing our clients with exceptional service. This is our differentiator in the marketplace. We're not just a home inspection company that does the inspection and then we disappear. We're a company that wants to build relationships, become a resource and serve our clients and customers any way we can, before, during and well after every inspection.

Expanding on that concept of collaborating with your competition, we've often found in our Realtor© workshops that the simple exercise of going around the room and inviting people to share what they like to do in their free time, is a great icebreaker. The simple reality is that you might know a lot of the Realtors© around you, but at the same time, they're technically your competition, trying to get listings or finding homes for buyers. But expanding that universe, breaking down some of those barriers, are ways of strengthening your overall positioning in the market, making you more resilient because you've created allies and you're giving each other support. Very often when we go around the room with the "what's your hobby" question, multiple people in the room will give the same answer. This gives you an avenue and an opening to start talking with each other about that thing you have in common.

Back to our experience at Waypoint. There's a member of MIC, another business owner who is in our direct area of operation. Technically they are our direct competition and are on essentially the same level we are in terms of service and the knowledge base that MIC provides. But the last time that we had a meeting with them it hit me that we're not competition. Although we may serve in the same area, we'll never have all the business. They will never have all the business. Why not work together and expand our influence because we are both companies who are out there to serve our clients and to provide them with the best quality and the best professional job possible? Why not work together and promote that type of servant leadership within the industry as a whole?

We're all in this together. We're all working towards similar goals. We're all trying to achieve our dreams; happiness, money, more time with family, whatever it may be. I believe that it's our duty to do what we can to help each other and to support each other as we're going through this journey.

Operate as a Team

Waypoint went from being a one-man operation to now having thirteen team members. As far as our company goes, or for really any business owner, it pays to remember you're not in it alone, you rely on a team to spring yourself forward and to grow your business. And to do that involves providing education, training, developing communication skills, and then getting your whole team on board so that you're working as one unit with the same mindset of servant leadership, in a way that sets you apart from your competition.

A big key to Waypoint's strength is that we're seen as a servant company focused on the wellbeing of our clients and Realtors©.

Anyone who works with Waypoint consistently on a daily, weekly or monthly basis knows they can call on us at any time. It doesn't matter the team member that is delivering, our clients and Realtors© know they will get the best product and the best service each and every time. Again, they confidently know who we are and what we are about. They know our *why* – caring through servant leadership.

When we are looking to add a new employee to our team, we try to find some of that *why* in them.

Our focus is on finding new team members that share our vision and goals. At the outset of our search we are looking for folks who share Waypoint's values.

Fundamentally, for home inspections there may be some state requirements that need to be met. There's formal training, and there are licensing tests. Those are the minimal expectations that just about anyone can meet. An additional factor we look for in candidates is the ability to talk with people from the heart instead of the head. It's not easy but it is something we try to train and instill in the folks that come to work with us. We learn their story and make sure that they're a good fit for our team.

So how do you grow your own team with a servant heart? Say a prospective employee comes to see you. You already know they need a job and pay check. You want to know what are the things that are really important to them, the things that make them act the way they act, feel the way they feel and do the things they do. It could be something as simple as they want more time with family, so they're looking for a job that has flexibility, or things like that. You're identifying their *why*.

When we're first training new members of the team and want them to learn communication skills and speaking from the heart, there's a lot of partnering with experienced members. There's also a lot of scripting to help them with the fundamentals. We encourage team members to add their own personalities into the scripting. "Here's the information you have to deliver, you must make sure that you cover these 21 points. Please use your personality when you're delivering it; we're not asking you to be a robot or impersonal." We role play with them until they are comfortable with their delivery. We take a similar approach in our presentations and meetings with Realtors©.

Another way we vet potential new team members is to see who can follow directions. When we reach out to people, we ask for a resume or curriculum vitae, along with at least 100 words of why they feel they would be a good fit for our company, and the top three things that are important to them in a customer-related environment. The main point of the 100-word and "top three" request is simply to see if they can follow directions. We'll put that out there, and each time we'll get numerous resumes, and only a few people will complete the 100-word and "top three" request of why they want to be a part of our company. What does that mean to those that didn't submit the extra requests? We're not even going to look at them because they're not following the directions.

Another tip is to ask people for stories. "Explain to me a time where you had a challenge, or explain to me a time where you worked on a team, what was your role?" Basically, that's the start, and then we go on from there.

CHAPTER 4: HOW TO CONNECT WITH YOUR CLIENTS

We're continuing on the theme of boosting your business in the real estate industry through the lens of servant leadership and meeting and exceeding your client expectations. Here are a few more secret weapons we've discovered, both from years of working in the industry ourselves and also from our increased involvement and partnerships with Realtors© as well as other home inspection businesses.

We have some more stories to share from that paradigm-shifting holiday in Belize, and parallels that struck us as ideal metaphors for continuing to grow into the million dollar business we're becoming. Also, we want you to be sure that when you partner with us, we're going to blow your clients away with the high caliber of our services, and make you look really good in the process!

Combine Excellence with Diplomacy

At one point in our holiday in Belize, we booked an excursion that included a cave tubing experience with a college graduate named Brian who was our guide. The tour involved the three of us Jeannette, Austin and me getting into inner tubes that were tied together to float down a river through a series of spectacular natural caves. Brian had a much smaller, more versatile inner tube and followed behind us, nudging us around each bend and telling us amazing stories that had to do with the region and the caves. Even though he was the expert in this region and the knowledgeable guide, he allowed us to go first and take it all in while he was content to nudge and lead from behind.

That's how we see our relationships with clients who are buying a house or a property. Even though we're experts in our area, full of knowledge and experience in the home buying industry, we allow our clients to see it and soak it in on their own while we're behind them, encouraging them through what we do for them, providing them information, providing them the understanding to help them make an informed decision. We lead them in the right direction but allow them to see the outcome; allow them to experience and to soak it in.

That's what our guide Brian was doing throughout the caves tour. He was behind us, he was slightly nudging us to the left or the right to keep us on course, but he was allowing us to look around and understand and soak it all in.

There were a few large tour groups of around 30 people on inner tubes also doing the cave tour. It was interesting to observe the different tour speeds. We got the slow, relaxed speed because there were three of us and we had our guide Brian to ourselves. Meanwhile, there were groups of 24 and 30 inner tubes led by guides from the tour companies and the cruise ships. They were going so fast they were probably creating a wake through the caves because they had to look at their watches. They had to get back to their ship. What were they experiencing?

A cruise ship coming to Belize cannot dock directly in the port because of the shallowness of the water. This means they have to dock about five miles off the coast and then take the smaller boats in and then catch buses to whatever tour they've chosen. And then it is an additional hour and a half to two hours of transit to get to the river and caves. It reminded us of the movie with Chevy Chase, 'European Vacation', where they had to rush around to see everything. Our more relaxed speed allowed us to better experience and develop a great relationship with our guide Brian, which none of us will forget.

This part of the Belize experience, the informative and relaxed river caves experience, emphasized to us the importance of developing relationships with our clients, ensuring they don't feel rushed through the home inspection process, making sure we don't commandeer their experience but at the same time being completely available to guide their experience, to answer their questions, to nudge them from behind.

This kind of servant leadership, nudging from behind, has all kinds of business applications. For example, just last week I had a conversation with a home inspector in New York City, who I'll call Jack. Jack has 12 years of experience in the industry, and he had been approached about joining up with another home inspector who had even more experience. He thought it might be a good idea because he's struggling to take the next step and build the business to a multi-inspector company rather than remaining a one-man shop. Jack knew I'd been in his position, before Waypoint's growth, just over three years ago, so he wanted my advice. The biggest thing I did was to listen to him. He was telling me about the relationship that he was developing with this other home inspector and how they were talking about joining forces and creating a company. As he was talking it became evident that this wasn't going to be a good partnership for him.

But I didn't tell him that outright, I just kept asking questions like, "What would you do if this were to happen? How do you see things evolving when it comes to making decisions, or training your team, or your style of operating?" We talked for a good hour, and in the end, Jack said, "You know what, Bob, I don't think this is going to be the right fit." I said, "Well I was reading that with your message, I don't think you should make that decision right away. I don't see your *whys* aligning. I encourage you to take your wife and family and go somewhere for a few days to clear your head and decide." But I also encouraged him, "Jack, I see it within you that you can do this on your own, you can build this on your own like I did."

I've had the same kind of conversation with other people, where I've had a role coaching and encouraging their business growth. I said to Jack, "The biggest issue you have, Jack, is that you can't get out of your own way fast enough, and once you understand that, you're going to do wonderful things."

I play a coaching role to a number of other inspectors, which works because I naturally like to help other people. And helping other people doesn't necessarily mean giving them the answers. Just like the story of Jack above, I will have a conversation with them and continue to ask questions and read between the lines. Through this, Waypoint as a business is transcending the home inspection aspect to encompass a broader role in the real estate industry.

During the trip to Belize we were all touched by the genuineness and sincerity we experienced on a daily basis from anybody that we came in contact with; whether it was at the resort or having something to eat or stopping to ask questions. With each encounter we felt like a good buddy was putting their arms around us and saying, "Instead of just telling you, let me show you." We returned from Belize with a renewed commitment to providing that same experience, whether dealing with home buyers or partnering with you, our valued Realtors©.

Write Hard and Talk Soft

We provide a very intensive on the job training program for our inspector trainees, in addition to the fundamentals of home inspection that they learn in school. Half the job that our inspectors need to learn to do really well is to be able to articulate their strong knowledge base onto a report for the clients. Again, that's half the job.

Initially, our inspectors will ride alongside a seasoned, experienced, inspector, usually with Eddy, our senior vice president of field operations. He works with the newer inspectors in the field, making sure they understand the technical aspects of the job and ensuring they can perform the inspection and put the results into a report in a way that is succinctly written and easy to understand for both clients and real estate agents. It's all about making sure the report has all the information that the client needs to make that fundamental decision on whether they want to continue to purchase that home.

The other half of the job is how our inspectors communicate with the clients. We've developed scripts, and we role play with those scripts as well. We have a checklist of things our inspectors must cover at an inspection, whether they're introducing themselves to the client, talking about what they can expect at the inspection, or providing information and describing our value-added services. There are a couple dozen points that they absolutely have to cover at the beginning of the inspection. How they relay that to the client is entirely dependent upon what type of personality they have. We allow them leeway to inject their personality as long as those items are covered.

The other aspect of communication with the client involves relaying the results of the inspection. If the client is present at the inspection, our inspectors walk them around the property. Then they show them everything on the report and are available to answer any questions.

We have a little saying: "Write hard and talk soft." "Write hard" means that we make sure everything is in the inspection report, and "talk soft" means explaining the report in a way that they'll fully understand it.

There are some clients out there who say something like, "Give it to me, I don't care what's wrong with the house. I love it. I'm going to buy it, I'm going to fix it." There are other people that the first little thing that concerns them means you've got to talk them back off the ledge. It all depends on what their temperament is like.

So while it's important to know how to take the information and put it on a report, it's just as important to be that communicator, be that teacher and be that educator with the client so they can make an educated decision on what they want to do next. For a person to be a successful inspector with Waypoint, this is what they have to do, and they have to do it well.

First time home buyers, in particular, might have a lot of concerns because there's a lot that they don't know about purchasing a home, or how the home functions. So we train our inspectors to communicate exactly what's going on. Just as in any other industry, home inspectors have their own lingo, and we make a point of making that relatable to our clients.

Equally as important as what's on the report is how it's presented to the client. With the home inspection, we're basically looking for two things. First, we're looking for major defects, things that are safety issues or that could become safety issues. Second, we're looking for the minor, more cosmetic issues; things that really shouldn't have any impact on a decision to purchase the home.

When it comes to major issues, our inspectors have gone through specialized training and understand how to communicate these effectively. Newer inspectors participate in ride-a-longs with other seasoned inspectors and learn a variety of communication styles. As the old cliché goes, we don't make mountains out of molehills. We try to ensure that if there is a genuine problem, it's communicated in a way that doesn't completely blow the deal.

At the same time, our job as a home inspector is to provide all the facts on that home. If there is a major issue with that house, whether it is a safety issue like a hazardous electrical panel or a roof at the end of its useful life, we make sure that our inspectors know how to communicate in a way that is clear and effective for the client. They make sure the client understands the nature of the issue and the seriousness of it. We also make sure that they explain it in a way that doesn't alarm the client. This is what we consider a 'charge neutral approach'.

We also encourage our inspectors to not just highlight all the issues, but also point out some of the good aspects of the home. Let's say the kitchen has been freshly renovated. The inspector might say, "Hey, I can see why you fell in love with this house. Look at this beautiful kitchen." For some clients, even if a house has some issues with it, it might still be the perfect home for them.

So it's our job to report on the issues in the home, but we're also trying to retain the sense that the buyer is the one making the final decision on whether they want to take on the necessary repairs. We try and keep it as neutral as we can because, at the end of the day, it's all going to come down to the buyer, what's in their mind, what they see as a deal breaker or what they see as something that they find manageable.

Offer a 200-Percent Guarantee

One of the other services we offer with every home inspection is our 200 percent satisfaction guarantee. That means that if a client is not satisfied with the inspection, we refund the cost of the inspection and we pay for another licensed inspector of their choice to come out do the inspection.

That might sound fairly fundamental, but it's made a big impact on our long-term connection with home buyers and our role in the industry in general. We noticed that some other companies were charging more for that type of service, whereas we regard this as a base value for the home inspection. So we're really proud of the caliber of service we provide.

In addition to that, on the client side of things, we will always be available to assist our clients with unforeseen issues that may arise after the inspection is completed.

For example, with one particular client, we completed an inspection on a bright and sunny day. There were insulated panels over the back patio and no apparent signs of active leaks. It just so happened that about two or three days after the inspection a tropical storm came through and the client realized that there was a leak in those insulated panels.

This client was new to the area, which meant he didn't really have any contractors or any roofers in the area that he knew to go to. So we took it upon ourselves to try and help him sort this issue out. We arranged for a contractor to complete an estimate so we could submit it to the warranty company and get everything taken care of for the client. This process dragged on because we went through contractor after contractor, roofer after roofer. They were either too busy to help us or gave us the runaround. We had one contractor who said, "Oh, we're going to have to tear apart the whole structure and build a whole new roof," which was completely out of budget.

We eventually did find somebody, after about a month of searching through companies, to come out and give us a reasonable estimate. Where the first contractor said it was going to have to be completely torn down and rebuilt, this other contractor came in and said, "I can do it for X amount of dollars," that was well within the client's budget.

We consider that part of our due diligence. We offer a higher level of personal service, and we're willing to go above and beyond for our clients. We're proud of it and happy that our company is in this position with a solid support system behind us. We strive to help clients and to build lifetime relationships with them.

Champion Causes in Your Community

Back to our holiday in Belize. On another day we flew from San Pedro to the mainland to visit a sanctuary for howler monkeys. At the sanctuary, we were met by Robert, an older gentleman who served as our guide for the day. Yet, he wasn't just a tour guide; by the time the day ended it felt like he was part of our family.

The sanctuary was created decades ago by individual landowners who saw the howler monkeys becoming endangered because their habitat was slowly disappearing. In Belize, in the northern part of the country, there are miles and miles of sugar cane fields. In the west, you have mountainous regions, and in the east, you have the flat plains. Years ago these landowners decided that along the back of their properties they would allow the trees to grow to build a continuous canopy. The howler monkeys could travel for miles and miles without ever having to touch the ground and leave their habitat.

These landowners had collaboratively agreed to do this to prevent the howler monkey from becoming endangered or possibly extinct. It impressed upon us again the concept that, even though most of society is all about the bottom line or the profit, money isn't everything. The way to succeed includes giving back to the community.

We always felt that supporting the community was going to be part of who we are, and this particular experience in Belize, seeing the preservation of howler monkey habitat, just emphasized that fact. With that in mind, we continue to be involved with a number of non-profit and community initiatives and it contributes to how we continue to grow and develop within our community.

In 2015 we held our tenth anniversary and in conjunction with our celebration party we also supported the local YMCA. Florida is the number one state, and the county we live in is the number one county in the entire country for toddler drowning deaths. There's water everywhere, yet sadly many kids never learn to swim. So a big part of our support of the YMCA is ensuring young children are taught how to swim.

Unbeknownst to us, a group of other small businesses got together and put together a scholarship for the local YMCA called the Bob Hintze/Waypoint Scholarship that provides swim lessons for the local disadvantaged children. This showed us that although we might start out initially helping in the community simply because we feel that it's a responsibility, as time goes on it becomes ingrained into our company ethos, and it comes from the heart.

We're also big advocates of a non-profit organization devoted to helping domestic violence victims. In fact, we've been doing that for a number of years now. The organization helps survivors get back on their feet and supports them through education, job search skill-building and helping basic supply needs.

We've also supported our local disabled veterans group. An inspector who joined us a few years ago, a military veteran, had a deep desire to help disabled vets be more active in sporting events. After working with us for a period of time, he pursued his calling working full time with disabled vets. We'd see photos online where he's out in the water helping a quadriplegic soldier water ski. It was just amazing, and we felt moved to get behind and support that initiative as well.

When it comes down to it, we're a home inspection company, but we could be a real estate team, we could be contractors or plumbers or electricians. It doesn't matter what our business is or what industry we're in, in the sense that the end goal is to be successful and give back to the community. We want to help others grow, to build up and support others. This concept also comes into play when we're talking about our vision to transcend being "just" a home inspection company and helping real estate professionals transcend "just" being a Realtor©.

At the end of the day, whatever you're doing, you're doing it to help build others up, to help support the people around you and help them reach their goals. It's this genuine involvement in the community that serves to establish your business in a greater way than ever before. Simply put, we care.

Build Lifelong Client Relationships

There are two types of people that we work with. We either work with real estate professionals or with clients who are either selling their home, buying their home or current homeowners. Our goal at Waypoint is to build lifelong relationships with our realtor partners and clients, just as we've experienced in our Millionaire Inspector Community.

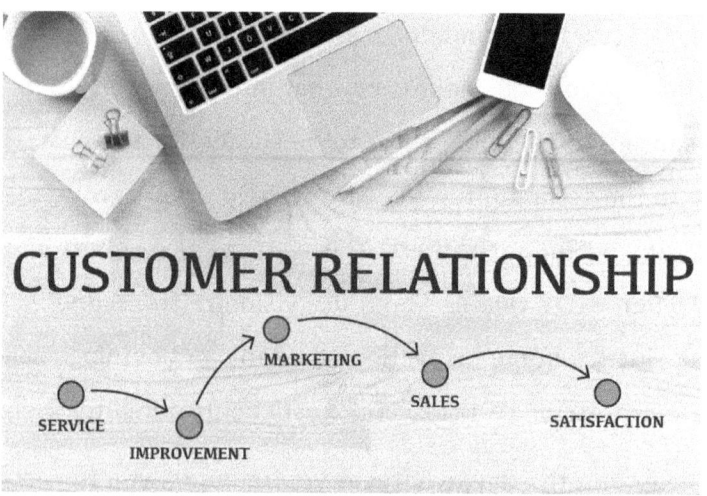

We're so much more than just inspectors. We're building lifetime relationships, and our clients can count on us for anything. We have products, services, and value-added items that basically will take them through the process of buying their house, inspecting their house and owning their house- feeling supported for years to come and knowing that they can always reach out to us.

We consider ourselves lifetime home consultants. That means that any period of time we are working with our clients, be it a day, a month, a year or five years after the inspection– whatever the period of time – we're always available to them.

Other inspection companies have different package structures with their home inspections (i.e., gold, silver and platinum) and they actually charge more for a client to get this type of ongoing service. But Waypoint provides this level of service to everyone, and we are committed to being a resource for any questions that our clients might have well into the future.

There are other home inspection companies that hand off the report, whether it's on-site or through email and that's it; you'll never be able to get a hold of them again. They'll never return a call. Their job is done.

That's not who Waypoint is. The important part of the job is building that lifetime relationship as long as the client wants us. That means we follow up our inspections with phone calls and emails. We might go over the big picture impressions of the property and then touch on a few things that the client needs to consider; maybe two or three bullet points. Then we send them the report so they can look through the detailed information. We encourage the client to come back to us as many times as they need to ensure that all their questions are answered.

A huge factor in building lifelong client relationships is that we are virtually reachable 24/7. That includes our inspector team as well. Our clients and our real estate partners know us for that. They know that they can call Bob, they can call Austin, they can call Eddy, and they can call Waypoint any day, anytime.

Conclusion

Bob: Life is a lesson. This book was written to document the road we have travelled and to offer others insight into a company that leads with a servant heart. It also serves as the foundation for Austin to build upon in the years to come. While we have demonstrated 'leading from behind' throughout the past 11 plus years, our trip to Belize in 2015 solidified our belief that the empowerment of others is the key to leading from behind. I am proud to have Austin as part of this great journey. He continues to absorb many lessons and opportunities and has become a strong leader in his own right. I hope to leave a legacy that identifies me as a leader with a servant heart, empowering others and always giving back to my community.

Austin: When I first started with Waypoint as one of two part-time Marketing Specialists, I didn't fully understand the impact that the job would have on me. Over the course of two years as I have grown into an ownership role, I have come to recognize and appreciate that impact. More than just the marketing position itself, I have learned the fundamentals of running a business that were not taught in any of my college classes. I am fortunate to be in a position that not many other people my age are in; a position where I am gaining actual hands-on experience and knowledge running a business. There's a stereotype of my generation that we want everything handed to us instead of working to achieve it on our own. I believe that I've personally broken through this stereotype through what I've contributed to the growth of Waypoint and also to our community. None of this would have been possible without the support of my dad (Bob) and uncle (Eddy). They've given me the opportunity to grow as a person while supporting the company, and for that I am forever grateful. I also am grateful for the support from the rest of my family including my mom (Jeannette) and aunt (Ivonnette).

We chose the title "It's Not About Me", because in 2013 we underwent a fundamental change in our business structure and mindset. Waypoint would no longer be a one man operation. We would focus on growing to serve our ever-expanding customer base. Just over three years ago we had one employee, me. Now we have thirteen team members committed to serving others and to being an integral part of our community. Our business continues to grow by leaps and bounds. Our team is focused on providing the absolute best service. Our customers and clients can depend on us at any time. It's not about me. Since Waypoint's founding in 2005, giving back to the community has been a main focus in how we operate. As we continue to grow exponentially we will be able to have even more of an impact on the lives of those around us.

There are many folks to thank for their input, support and encouragement as we wrote this book. Coaches Mike Crow, Jase Souder and AJ Puedan who continue to bring out our best. The MIC Platinum Excel team and Jeff Donaldson for challenging us to always be at our best. Ken Sherman whose expertise enabled our ideas and thoughts to make it to these pages. Partner Eddy Lai and our Waypoint team for always striving to put forth the best service. And finally, to our families for their overwhelming love, patience and support.

Acknowledgments

Mike Crow and his MIC team for their unwavering commitment to the inspection community, by constantly challenging us to expand our abilities- and to help each other.

Jase Souder, another great partner who's helping us with our ability to get in front of all different kinds of audiences which is, I feel the next generation of our company.

Ken Sherman has worked hard to support our creative process in writing this book from start to finish. Without him, the words would still be in our heads and not in this book.

And finally, thank you to the wonderful real estate agents and clients who we have the privilege of working with each day.

Contact the Authors

Website: <www.waypointwest.com>.

Email: <bob@waypointinspection.com>

<austin@waypointinspection.com>

Phone: 813- 486-8551

www.ingramcontent.com/pod-product-compliance
Lightning Source LLC
Chambersburg PA
CBHW061200180526
45170CB00002B/881